Painting on
Glass Stones
Tips & Techniques
for Fabulous Fun!

Illustrated by Raffaella Dowling

Text by Jessica Dowling

Photography by F. William Lagaret

Mud Puddle Books
NEW YORK

Painting on Glass Stones
Illustrated by Raffaella Dowling
Text by Jessica Dowling
Photography by F. William Lagaret

© 2006 by Mud Puddle Books, Inc.

Mud Puddle Books, Inc.
54 W. 21st Street
Suite 601
New York, NY 10010
info@mudpuddlebooks.com

ISBN: 1-59412-152-4

Designed by Tasha Sakhrani

Printed and bound in China

Contents

Introduction   4
Materials   7
Holiday   8
Hearts   9
Sky   10
Flowers   11
Abstracts   12
Dots   14
Animals   16
Bugs   17
Circles   18
Ocean   19
Sports   20
Faces   21
Black & White   22
Rainbow   23
Pluid   24
Food   25
Alphabet   26
Tips & Techniques   28
Sketching Area   30

Painting on glass stones to make your own

All you need to get started is a glass stone, some paint, a brush and your own imagination. Remember, the technique used to paint on the glass is very different from the technique you would normally use to paint on a surface…in fact, it is the exact opposite!

The glass stone has two sides: one rounded, and one flat. You paint the flat side, wait for it to dry, and then view your design from the rounded side. This magnifies the design you've made and gives it a unique look. Here's the catch: you have to paint the foreground first and the background last.

For instance, if you were painting a glass stone to look like a smiley face, you would first paint the mouth and the eyes. After waiting for this to dry completely, you would then paint the background color of the face. When this dries, you flip it around to reveal your reverse-painted work of art! Once you get used to it, it is a very simple technique.

is a fun and easy way miniature treasures!

There is no need to paint complicated subjects. Because of the way the stone magnifies and intensifies your design, even a simple pattern of stripes or dots painted on the stone will look great! Glass stones are the perfect medium to try abstract art.

Keep in mind everything that you paint on the back of the glass stone will appear in reverse when you flip it over! If you want to paint a letter, make sure you paint it backwards on the flat side of the rock.

If you make a mistake with a glass stone, don't worry! Drop the painted stone in a cup of warm water for a few minutes. This will loosen the paint. Then, using a sponge, scrub your design off the glass stone. Make sure you use a sponge that isn't being used to clean dishes or other food

utensils. Dry your stone with paper towels and start over! When you have assembled a collection of painted glass stones, there are many things you can do with them. They make great gifts for parents, teachers, or anyone else! By cutting a piece of self-adhesive magnetic backing (available at craft stores) to fit the back of a painted stone, you can make a set of unique, colorful magnets. A painted glass stone hot-glued to a flat thumbtack makes an original pushpin for a bulletin board. Even something as simple as arranging your stones on a desk or table will look great!

They make great gifts!

Materials

❋ **Acrylic Paint -** A good starter set would contain white, black, red, blue and yellow paint. You can mix these basic paints to create colors like purple, pink, and green. Fine arts acrylics cost a little more than craft acrylics but provide a much thicker coat of paint. This can lessen the amount of coats you have to apply when painting on a clear surface.

❋ **Very fine acrylic brushes -** Sizes 0 and 1 work well because the surface you are painting is so small.

❋ **Toothpicks -** When painting glass stones, these can work just as well as brushes!

❋ **A cup of water** to clean brushes.

❋ **Paper towels** for surface cleanup.

❋ **Newspaper** to lay on top of your work area to protect surfaces.

HEARTS

SKY

FLOWERS

TIP

Always remember—
when painting glass
stones, you paint
"in reverse"!
This means the
foreground goes
on first, and the
background last!

ABSTRACTS

TIP

A little paint goes a long way! Put only a dab of each color on your palette. You can always add more.

DOTS

15

ANIMALS

BUGS

CIRCLES

OCEAN

TIP

Make sure to take
a break from
painting every so
often to give your
hands and eyes
a rest.

19

SPORTS

FACES

BLACK & WHITE

22

RAINBOW

PLAID

FOOD

ALPHABET

More Great Tips!

Try to think of creative backgrounds for your subject matter. Don't always use white! Try bright colors, stripes, or even polka dots as a backdrop for your creations.

If you decide you don't like a finished glass stone, soak it for a while in a glass of hot water, and rub the paint off with a dry paper towel.

Try not to water down the paint too much. The thicker the paint, the better it will adhere to the glass.

Change the water you use to clean your brushes often, to prevent muddy colors.

Don't leave brushes in your cup of water! This can cause the bristles and handle of your brush to get ruined. After washing your brushes, lay them on some paper towels to dry until you need them again. Well cared for brushes can last years!

After your designs are completely dry, give the underside of the glass stone a coat of clear acrylic to prevent your design from rubbing off.

Good lighting conditions are key! Make sure you are working in bright light. This will allow you to see colors clearly, and keep your eyes from working too hard.

Toothpicks are one of the most useful tools for painting glass stones. Dipping one in a small amount of paint allows you to create fine details and designs.

Use this area to sketch some of your own ideas for painting stones!

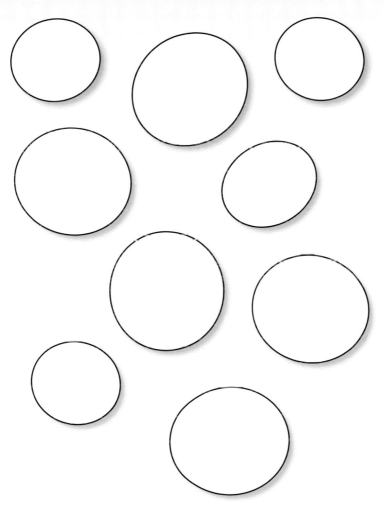

I

GLASS STONES